The Most Amazing Hockey Stories of All Time for Kids

15 Incredible Tales From Hockey History for Young Readers

Bradley Simon

TABLE OF CONTENTS

CHAPTER 1
The Miracle on Ice: A David and Goliath Story

In the winter of 1980, a remarkable event unfolded in the small town of Lake Placid, New York. It was during the Winter Olympics, a stage where athletes from around the world showcased their talents and dedication. This story, known as the "Miracle on Ice," is about an extraordinary hockey game that transcended the boundaries of sports, becoming a symbol of determination, teamwork, and the indomitable spirit of underdogs.

To fully appreciate this moment in history, we need to understand the landscape of hockey at that time. Hockey is more than a game; it's a dynamic sport that demands skill, strategy, and heart. It's a global passion, but in the late 1970s and early 1980s, two countries stood out in the hockey world: the United States and the Soviet Union.

The Soviet Union's hockey team was a formidable force. Adorned in their signature red jerseys, they were the reigning champions, having clinched the gold medal in the four previous Winter Olympics. These players were not just athletes; they were virtuosos of the sport, playing with a precision and skill that seemed almost otherworldly. Their game was a blend of art and athleticism, a display of hockey at its finest.

Contrast this with the United States hockey team. Imagine a group of young college athletes, fresh-faced and eager, each with a personal story and a shared love for hockey. Unlike the seasoned professionals of the Soviet team, these were amateur players, some still honing their skills on the ice. They were students of the game, in every sense of the word.

Guiding this team was Herb Brooks, a coach renowned for his tough approach and innovative tactics. Brooks saw potential where others saw inexperience. He believed in the power of hard work, discipline, and teamwork. He envisioned these young players not just competing against the best but also standing a chance to win.

The road to the Olympics was challenging for the US team. It involved rigorous training sessions, learning to function as a cohesive unit, and overcoming the mental and physical demands of the sport. They entered the competition as underdogs, a term in sports for those expected to be outmatched and defeated. However, the heart of an underdog beats with the hope of achieving the impossible.

The US team's commitment was unyielding. They trained relentlessly, each player contributing his unique strengths – speed, agility, resilience. Under Brooks' guidance, they began to evolve, becoming more than just a team; they became a unified force on the ice.

Before the Olympics, the team faced the Soviet Union in an exhibition match. It was a sobering encounter, as the Soviets dominated the game, winning with a significant margin. Many saw this as a preview of what was to come – a confirmation of the Soviet team's invincibility.

But the true essence of sports lies in its unpredictability and the relentless spirit of its players. That defeat was not an end but a catalyst for the US team. It ignited a determination to rise to the occasion, to face their formidable opponents once more, this time on the grand stage of the 1980 Winter Olympics.

The excitement of the Olympics was infectious. Athletes from diverse nations gathered, each representing their country's hopes and aspirations. The US team, with their newfound confidence, advanced through the tournament, surpassing expectations and reaching the semi-finals. Here, they would face the Soviet Union again, setting the scene for an unforgettable chapter in sports history.

The stage was set for a monumental clash. The young, spirited US team against the seasoned, seemingly invincible Soviet squad. It was the classic underdog story, but the outcome of this confrontation was far from written in the stars.

As the semi-final match approached, the atmosphere in Lake Placid was electric. Fans from across the globe, and especially those from the United States, filled the stands, their excitement and anticipation palpable. The young American team stepped onto the ice, facing not just their opponents, but also the weight of history and expectation.

The Soviet Union team, confident and experienced, was expected to dominate. Their style of play was like a well-oiled machine, each player moving with purpose and precision. Their track record spoke for itself – they were not just participants in the Olympics; they were the gold standard.

On the other side, the American team, led by Coach Brooks, was a mix of nerves and excitement. These players, some of whom were still in their teens, were about to face the toughest challenge of their young careers. They knew the eyes of their nation, and indeed the world, were on them.

The game started with the Soviets asserting their dominance early on. They moved swiftly, their passes sharp and accurate, a display of skill and coordination honed through years of playing together. The American team, in contrast, seemed to be finding their footing, their movements initially hesitant under the immense pressure.

However, as the minutes ticked by, something remarkable began to happen. The young American team started to adapt, to respond to the pace and style of their opponents. They weren't just there to participate; they were there to compete. Their skating became more confident, their passes crisper, and slowly, they began to challenge the Soviet team.

The crowd played its part too. The chants and cheers of "USA! USA!" echoed through the arena, a tidal wave of support and belief. This encouragement seemed to fuel the American players, each stride, each shot infused with a growing confidence.

Throughout the game, the lead swung back and forth. The Soviet team scored, showcasing their legendary skill, but the Americans answered back. Each goal by the US team was more than just a point on the scoreboard; it was a statement of resilience, a testament to their spirit and hard work.

As the final period of the game began, the score was close, much closer than many had anticipated. The Soviets, perhaps for the first time, looked fallible, their invincibility in question. The Americans, on the other hand, were playing the best hockey of their lives. They were no longer just a team of college students; they were Olympians, representing their country on the biggest stage.

The tension in the arena was almost tangible. Every pass, every shot, every save was met with a collective gasp or cheer. The players on the ice were acutely aware that these moments would define their careers, their lives, and in some ways, the very spirit of their nation.

Then, in a moment that seemed to defy belief, the American team scored, taking the lead against the mighty Soviet Union. The crowd erupted, a mixture of joy, disbelief, and pride filling the arena. The final minutes of the game were a blur of emotions, the American players defending their lead with everything they had.

As the clock ticked down to zero, the impossible had been achieved. The United States had defeated the Soviet Union, the unbeatable team, in what would be remembered as one of the greatest upsets in sports history. The players embraced, their faces a mixture of exhaustion and elation, their victory a testament to the belief that anything is possible.

The "Miracle on Ice" was more than just a game. It was a story of David triumphing over Goliath, a lesson in the power of belief and the spirit of determination. It showed that with hard work, unity, and an unyielding spirit, even the most daunting challenges can be overcome.

As the final buzzer sounded, signaling the end of the game, the arena erupted in a symphony of cheers and applause. The players on the American team, young and filled with exuberance, were overcome with emotion. They had done the unthinkable, defeating a team that many had considered invincible. This was not just a victory in a game of hockey; it was a triumph of the human spirit.

In the midst of the celebration, Coach Herb Brooks stood on the sidelines, a proud but composed figure. He had pushed his team, believed in them, and led them to one of the greatest moments in sports history. His vision of bringing together a group of college players and molding them into a team capable of taking on the world's best had been realized.

The impact of this victory resonated far beyond the ice rink in Lake Placid. Across the United States, people celebrated, feeling a sense of unity and pride. In a time when the country was facing various challenges, both domestically and internationally, this triumph served as a beacon of hope and joy.

For the players, this game was the culmination of months of rigorous training, of learning to work together, to trust each other, and to believe in themselves. They had faced doubts from others and perhaps even from within, but they had persevered. Each player had contributed to this victory, their individual stories woven into the fabric of this historic achievement.

The Soviet team, gracious in defeat, acknowledged the skill and determination of their opponents. They had been the champions for so long, their dominance in the sport almost a foregone conclusion. This loss, while unexpected, was a reminder of the unpredictable nature of sports and the potential for surprises.

As the news of the victory spread, it captured the imagination of people around the world. The story of the underdog, the team that had defied odds, became an inspiration. It was a reminder that in sports, as in life, anything is possible with hard work, dedication, and belief.

The aftermath of the "Miracle on Ice" was significant. The United States team advanced to the finals of the Olympic tournament, their confidence at an all-time high. The victory over the Soviet Union had given them the belief that they could achieve even more. And they did, going on to win the gold medal, a crowning glory to their incredible journey.

For many of the players on the team, this game was the highlight of their hockey careers. They became heroes, not just in the world of sports, but to anyone who heard their story. They showed that with teamwork, commitment, and a never-say-die attitude, even the most daunting obstacles can be overcome.

Years later, the "Miracle on Ice" continues to be a source of inspiration. It stands as a testament to the power of sports to unite, to inspire, and to transform. It is a story that transcends national boundaries and speaks to the universal human qualities of courage, determination, and the will to succeed against all odds.

CHAPTER 2
Gretzky's Greatness: Breaking Records, Breaking Barriers

In the world of hockey, there are many stars, but there is one name that shines brighter than all the rest: Wayne Gretzky. Known as "The Great One," Gretzky's journey in hockey is not just a story of breaking records; it's a tale of passion, dedication, and redefining the very essence of the game.

Wayne Gretzky was born on January 26, 1961, in Brantford, Ontario, Canada. From a very young age, it was clear that Gretzky had a special connection with hockey. His love for the game was evident, and his talent was extraordinary. He wasn't the biggest or the strongest player, but what he lacked in size, he more than made up for in skill, intelligence, and determination.

Gretzky started skating at the tender age of two, and by the time he was six, he was playing with ten-year-olds. His ability to read the game, to anticipate where the puck would be, was almost magical. He had a knack for being in the right place at the right time, a skill that would become a hallmark of his play.

As Gretzky grew older, his love for hockey only intensified. He spent hours on the rink, practicing and honing his skills. It wasn't just about physical training; Gretzky studied the game, understanding its nuances, learning from both his successes and his failures. He was a student of hockey, always looking to improve, always pushing the boundaries of what was possible.

When Gretzky entered the world of professional hockey, he brought a new level of excitement and skill to the game. He began his NHL career in 1979 with the Edmonton Oilers, and from the very start, it was clear that he was a different kind of player. Gretzky's style was unique – he was more of a playmaker than a traditional scorer. He had an uncanny ability to create opportunities, to make plays that others couldn't even see.

Gretzky's impact on the game was immediate and profound. In his first season, he won the Hart Trophy as the league's most valuable player, a feat he would repeat several times throughout his career. His presence on the ice was transformative; he made not just himself but his entire team better.

But Gretzky's greatness wasn't just in his individual skill; it was in his ability to redefine the game of hockey. He played with a creativity and a vision that had never been seen before. He thought about hockey in a way that was different, seeing passes and plays that no one else could. He wasn't just playing the game; he was changing it.

One of the most remarkable aspects of Gretzky's career was his ability to break records. He shattered them with a frequency and ease that was astonishing. From the most goals in a season to the most assists, Gretzky's name became synonymous with hockey excellence. His records were not just numbers; they were symbols of his unmatched talent and dedication to the sport.

However, Gretzky's journey wasn't without challenges. In the world of sports, where physicality and strength are often prized, Gretzky's style was initially seen as unconventional. He wasn't the typical hockey player; he didn't overpower his opponents with force. Instead, he outsmarted them, using his intelligence and skill to navigate the ice.

Gretzky's approach to hockey was like a chess master playing on ice. He was always two steps ahead, anticipating the moves of his opponents, and setting up plays that seemed impossible. This strategic mindset was one of his greatest assets, making him not just a player to watch, but a player to learn from.

As Gretzky's fame grew, so did the attention on him. Fans filled stadiums, eager to witness his magic on the ice. His jersey, number 99, became iconic, a symbol of excellence in hockey. Young players around the world looked up to him, dreaming of one day emulating his achievements.

But with fame comes pressure, and Gretzky handled it with grace and humility. He was aware of his influence on the sport and the responsibility that came with it. He became a role model, not just for his skill, but for his sportsmanship, his dedication, and his love for the game.

One of the most significant moments in Gretzky's career came in 1988 when he was traded from the Edmonton Oilers to the Los Angeles Kings. This move was more than just a transfer of a player; it was a shift in the hockey world. Gretzky's arrival in Los Angeles brought hockey to the forefront in a region where it hadn't been popular. He not only introduced the sport to new fans but also helped it grow in places where it had previously been overlooked.

Gretzky's impact on the Kings was transformative. He led the team to new heights, including their first Stanley Cup Finals appearance in 1993. His presence in Los Angeles changed the landscape of hockey in the United States, increasing its popularity and inspiring a new generation of players.

Throughout his career, Gretzky continued to break records, each one a testament to his enduring skill and passion. He became the all-time leading scorer in NHL history, a record many thought unachievable. But for Gretzky, it wasn't just about setting records; it was about pushing the limits of what was possible in hockey.

Gretzky's greatness extended beyond the rink. He was known for his kindness, his willingness to engage with fans, and his commitment to promoting the sport. He understood the power of hockey to bring people together, to create moments of joy and inspiration.

As Gretzky's career progressed, he began to be recognized not just as a great player, but as one of the greatest athletes of all time. His influence on hockey was compared to that of Michael Jordan in basketball or Babe Ruth in baseball – transcendent, enduring, and unparalleled.

Despite all his achievements, Gretzky remained grounded. He never forgot the love for hockey that had driven him from a young age. He continued to play with the same joy and passion that had marked his early days on the rink in Brantford. His love for the game was infectious, inspiring those around him to strive for their best.

Gretzky's legacy is not just in the records he set or the games he won. It's in the way he played the game, with creativity, intelligence, and a deep respect for the sport. He showed that greatness in hockey isn't just about physical strength; it's about vision, strategy, and heart.

As Gretzky continued to dazzle fans and rewrite the record books, he began to cement his legacy as more than just a phenomenal player. He became a symbol of the sport itself, embodying the very best of what hockey could offer – skill, sportsmanship, and a relentless pursuit of excellence.

Wayne Gretzky's influence reached far beyond the NHL. He became involved in international hockey, representing

Canada in several world championships and the Winter Olympics. His presence on the international stage further solidified his status as a global ambassador for the sport. Young players from different countries looked up to him, seeing in Gretzky a model of what they could aspire to become.

One of the most admirable qualities of Gretzky was his team-first mentality. Despite all his individual records and accolades, he always emphasized the importance of teamwork and collaboration. He knew that hockey was not just about one player, but about the collective effort of the entire team. This philosophy was evident in the way he played – always looking to set up a teammate, to create opportunities for others, and to make the players around him better.

Gretzky's approach to the game was also marked by a constant desire to learn and adapt. Even as he reached the pinnacle of his career, he continued to evolve his playstyle, adapting to new challenges and opponents. This adaptability was a key factor in his sustained success and longevity in the sport.

As Gretzky's career neared its end, the hockey world began to reflect on his immense impact. He had not just broken records; he had expanded the horizons of what was possible in hockey. He had brought the game to new audiences, inspired countless players, and left an indelible mark on the sport.

In 1999, Wayne Gretzky retired from professional hockey, leaving behind a legacy unmatched in the sport. His final game was an emotional moment, not just for him but for all who had followed his career. Fans and players alike recognized that they were witnessing the end of an era, the conclusion of a journey that had transformed hockey.

Gretzky's retirement was followed by numerous honors and accolades. His number 99 was retired league-wide by the NHL, an unprecedented gesture that spoke to his unique impact on the sport. He was inducted into the Hockey Hall of Fame, and his records stood as lofty benchmarks for future generations.

But perhaps the greatest testament to Gretzky's greatness is the way he is remembered and revered. Stories of his exploits on the ice are passed down from generation to generation, not just as tales of athletic prowess but as lessons in dedication, innovation, and the pursuit of dreams.

Wayne Gretzky's journey from a young boy skating on a backyard rink in Brantford to the pinnacle of hockey greatness is a source of inspiration. It reminds us that with passion, hard work, and a willingness to think differently, barriers can be broken, and new heights can be reached.

CHAPTER 3
The Goalie Who Changed the Game: Manon Rhéaume's Historic Debut

In the world of sports, there are moments that break barriers and change the game forever. One such moment belongs to Manon Rhéaume, a trailblazing goaltender who made history not just in hockey, but in the world of sports. This is her story, a story of determination, courage, and breaking glass ceilings.

Manon Rhéaume was born on February 24, 1972, in Lac Beauport, Quebec, Canada. From a young age, Manon was drawn to the thrill and excitement of hockey, a sport that captivated the hearts of many in her country. Unlike most young girls who aspired to figure skating or other sports, Manon had her eyes set on the hockey net. She wanted to be a goaltender, a position both critical and challenging in the game of hockey.

Goalkeeping in hockey is not for the faint-hearted. It requires agility, quick reflexes, and the bravery to face off against rubber pucks flying at high speeds. Manon, from her early days on the ice, showed she had not just the skill, but the heart to guard the goal. She played with a determination that belied her age, diving for saves and standing tall against her opponents.

As she grew older, Manon's passion for hockey only intensified. She played in various leagues, often being the only girl on the team. While this could have been daunting, Manon saw it as a challenge. She wanted to prove that she could play at the same level as the boys, that her talent and dedication were what mattered most on the ice.

In 1992, something remarkable happened – something that would etch Manon Rhéaume's name in the annals of sports history. She was invited to the training camp for the Tampa Bay Lightning, an NHL team. This was unprecedented, a moment that shattered the conventional boundaries in the world of sports. Manon was about to become the first woman to play in one of the four major North American professional sports leagues.

Imagine the scene at the training camp. There were seasoned players, veterans of the sport, and then there was Manon – a young woman in a male-dominated world, about to make her mark. The pressure was immense, the spotlight intense, but Manon was not deterred. She laced up her skates, donned her goalie gear, and stepped onto the ice with a composure that spoke volumes.

Manon's debut in a preseason game for the Tampa Bay Lightning was a groundbreaking moment. When she guarded the net, it wasn't just about stopping pucks; it was about breaking down barriers, challenging stereotypes, and opening doors for future generations. She faced shots from professional players, some of whom were the best in the league, and she stood her ground.

Her performance was more than just respectable; it was inspiring. She showed that talent and hard work know no gender. Manon's presence in the net sent a powerful message – that a woman could compete in a male-dominated sport and succeed.

The impact of Manon's debut reached far beyond the ice rink. It was a moment of empowerment for young girls everywhere, an example that they could aspire to and achieve anything they set their hearts on. Manon Rhéaume had become a symbol of possibility, a beacon of hope for equality in sports.

Manon Rhéaume's journey in hockey, however, was not just a smooth path to success. She faced challenges and obstacles along the way, some that tested her resolve and passion for the sport. Being the first woman in a male-dominated arena meant dealing with skepticism and doubt, not just from fans and media but sometimes from fellow players too.

Despite these hurdles, Manon continued to pursue her dream with unwavering determination. Each time she stepped onto the ice, whether it was for a practice or a game, she did so with the knowledge that she was paving the way for others. She was not just playing for herself; she was playing for every young girl who had been told that hockey was not for them.

Manon's skill as a goaltender was undeniable. She had quick reflexes, a keen sense of the game, and the ability to make split-second decisions under pressure. Her style of goalkeeping was a blend of art and athleticism, a dance on ice where each move was critical.

Beyond her physical abilities, what set Manon apart was her mental strength. Goalkeeping in hockey can be a solitary experience, with the weight of the game often resting on the goalie's shoulders. Manon embraced this challenge, showing a level of focus and resilience that inspired both her teammates and her fans.

As Manon continued her career, she became more than just a player; she became an advocate for women in sports. She spoke about the importance of equality, the need for opportunities for women athletes, and the power of sport to bring about change. Her story was not just about breaking a barrier; it was about starting a conversation on how sports could be more inclusive and diverse.

Manon's impact extended to the younger generation, inspiring countless girls to take up hockey and pursue their dreams in sports. She showed them that their gender did not define their capabilities or limit their potential. Through her perseverance and success, she opened doors that had previously been closed, creating opportunities for future female athletes.

The legacy of Manon Rhéaume in the world of hockey is profound. She changed the game, not just in the way it was played, but in who could play it. Her historic debut in the NHL was a defining moment, challenging perceptions and setting a new standard for what was possible.

Years after her groundbreaking game, Manon's influence remains strong. She is a role model, a symbol of progress, and a testament to the enduring spirit of sportsmanship and equality. Her story is a reminder that with courage and conviction, barriers can be broken, and new paths can be forged.

Manon Rhéaume's story is not just about hockey; it's about challenging the status quo, about believing in oneself, and about the relentless pursuit of one's dreams. It's a story that resonates with anyone who has ever faced doubt or discrimination and has chosen to rise above it.

Manon Rhéaume's presence on the ice during her historic NHL debut was not just a personal triumph; it was a pivotal moment in sports history that resonated across the world. It broke long-standing gender barriers and set a precedent that challenged the norms of not only hockey but all sports.

After her time with the Tampa Bay Lightning, Manon continued to pursue her passion for hockey. She played for various teams, both in men's leagues and women's leagues, always showcasing her exceptional skills and inspiring spirit. Her journey through different teams and leagues further highlighted her resilience and adaptability, traits that are essential for any athlete.

One of the remarkable aspects of Manon's career was her participation in the 1998 Winter Olympics, the first time women's ice hockey was included in the Olympic Games. Representing Canada, Manon once again took her place in goal, defending her team on the world's biggest sports stage. This was a moment of great pride and significance, not just for Manon but for all those who had followed her journey.

In the Olympics, Manon demonstrated the same remarkable talent and determination that had marked her entire career. She played with a blend of grace and grit, showcasing the skills that had taken her from the ponds of Quebec to the Olympic arena. Her performance was a testament to her enduring love for the game and her commitment to excellence.

Manon's impact on hockey is reflected in the increased visibility and popularity of women's hockey. She played a crucial role in bringing attention to the sport, showing that women's hockey was exciting, competitive, and deserving of a global audience. Her legacy is seen in the growth of women's hockey programs, in the rising number of young girls lacing up skates and hitting the ice, and in the greater recognition of women's achievements in sports.

Off the ice, Manon became a spokesperson for gender equality in sports. She shared her experiences and insights, encouraging young athletes to pursue their dreams regardless of gender. Her message was clear: talent and hard work should be the only factors that determine one's ability to play and succeed in any sport.

Manon Rhéaume's story is more than just a series of games and achievements. It's a narrative of breaking down walls, of challenging and changing perceptions, and of inspiring the next generation. Her journey shows the power of dreams and the impact one person can have in altering the course of history.

CHAPTER 4
The Legend of Bobby Orr:
The Flying Goal

Certain moments in hockey history stand out as timeless, capturing the essence of the sport in a single play. One such moment is the legendary flying goal by Bobby Orr, a player whose name is synonymous with brilliance in the world of hockey. Bobby Orr wasn't just a player; he was a phenomenon, a defenseman who transformed the way the game was played.

Born in Parry Sound, Ontario, Canada, on March 20, 1948, Bobby Orr grew up in a world where hockey was more than just a sport; it was a way of life. From a young age, Orr showed an exceptional talent for the game, especially for a position as demanding and crucial as defense. What set Orr apart was not just his skill with the puck or his ability to read the game but his extraordinary skating ability.

In a sport where speed and agility are paramount, Orr's skating was poetry in motion. He had the rare ability to glide across the ice with grace and speed, making complex maneuvers look effortless. His style of play was revolutionary; he brought an offensive dynamism to a position traditionally focused on defense.

Orr's journey to becoming a hockey legend began when he joined the Boston Bruins in 1966. At that time, the Bruins were not the powerhouse team they are known as today. They were struggling, in need of a spark to reignite their competitive spirit. Bobby Orr became that spark and so much more.

From the moment he stepped onto the ice in a Bruins jersey, Orr began to redefine the role of a defenseman. He was everywhere on the ice – blocking shots, making tackles, and then, in the blink of an eye, leading an attack. His ability to transition from defense to offense was groundbreaking, changing the way teams played the game.

Orr's impact on the Bruins was immediate and profound. He helped transform the team into one of the most formidable in the NHL. Fans flocked to the games, eager to witness Orr's brilliance. He wasn't just a player; he was an icon, a symbol of skill and innovation in hockey.

One of the most remarkable aspects of Orr's career was his ability to score goals, a rare skill for a defenseman. He had an uncanny sense for finding the back of the net, a talent that culminated in one of the most famous goals in hockey history – the flying goal.

The flying goal occurred during the 1970 Stanley Cup Finals between the Boston Bruins and the St. Louis Blues. It was a moment that transcended the sport, a blend of skill, timing, and sheer athletic beauty. Orr received a pass, skated through the defense, and shot the puck past the goaltender. The moment the puck hit the net, Orr leaped into the air in a moment of pure joy and celebration. It was a goal that symbolized victory, not just for the Bruins, who won the Stanley Cup, but for the sport of hockey.

This iconic image of Orr flying through the air, arms outstretched, with the crowd erupting in celebration, is etched in the memory of hockey fans around the world. It was more than just a winning goal; it was a testament to Orr's incredible skill and the sheer joy of the game.

The image of Bobby Orr soaring through the air after scoring the Stanley Cup-winning goal is not just a snapshot of a triumphant moment; it captures the essence of Orr's playing style – fearless, dynamic, and always pushing the limits. This goal wasn't just a high point in Orr's career; it was a defining moment in the history of hockey, showcasing the potential of skill, determination, and creativity.

Orr's influence on the game went beyond his remarkable ability to score and defend. He brought a new level of excitement to hockey, captivating fans with his speed, agility, and intelligence on the ice. He played the game with a passion and a sense of freedom that inspired his teammates and thrilled spectators.

In every game, Orr displayed an unmatched combination of athleticism and strategy. He was a master at reading the play, anticipating his opponents' moves, and making split-second decisions. His hockey IQ was off the charts, allowing him to be always one step ahead of everyone else on the ice.

But what truly made Orr stand out was his leadership and sportsmanship. He was a team player through and through, always putting the success of the team above his own. He led by example, inspiring his teammates with his work ethic, humility, and dedication to the game.

Orr's impact on the Boston Bruins was transformative. He helped lead the team to two Stanley Cup victories, in 1970 and 1972, bringing joy and pride to the city of Boston. Under his influence, the Bruins became a symbol of excellence in hockey, a team that combined skill, teamwork, and the sheer joy of playing the game.

Off the ice, Orr was equally admired. He was known for his kindness, generosity, and commitment to his community. He understood the responsibility that came with being a role model and embraced it, using his platform to inspire and make a positive impact.

Throughout his career, Orr received numerous awards and accolades, reflecting his extraordinary contributions to the sport. He won the Norris Trophy as the league's best defenseman eight times, a record that speaks volumes about his talent and influence on the game.

However, Orr's career was not without challenges. Injuries, particularly to his knees, were a constant battle.

Despite the pain and the risk, Orr continued to play with the same intensity and passion, never letting his physical limitations diminish his love for the game.

Bobby Orr's legacy in hockey is enduring. He redefined what it meant to be a defenseman, blending defense and offense in a way that had never been seen before. He elevated the game of hockey, bringing it to new heights and leaving an indelible mark on the sport.

Bobby Orr's journey in hockey is a tale of not just athletic prowess, but also of pioneering a new way to approach the game. His style of play, marked by a blend of offensive and defensive skills, set a new standard for future generations of defensemen. He was not just a player; he was an innovator, constantly challenging the traditional roles and strategies in hockey.

As Orr's career progressed, his influence extended beyond the Boston Bruins and the NHL. He became a symbol of excellence in hockey, respected and admired by players and fans alike. His jersey, number 4, became iconic, representing not just a player, but an ideal of how the game could be played.

The legacy of Bobby Orr is also reflected in the way he inspired young players. Children who watched him play were mesmerized by his skills and motivated by his dedication. He showed them that with hard work and passion, the conventional limits of any position or role could be surpassed.

Orr's impact on hockey was about more than just his goals, assists, or awards. It was about the excitement and joy he brought to the game. He played hockey with a sense of wonder and enthusiasm that was contagious, reminding everyone why they loved the sport.

One of the most admirable aspects of Orr's character was his humility. Despite his fame and success, he remained grounded and approachable. He was always ready to share his knowledge and experience, whether it was with a young fan seeking an autograph or a rookie player looking for advice.

Orr's influence continued even after he hung up his skates. He became involved in various charitable activities, using his fame to support causes close to his heart. He also remained a respected figure in the hockey community, offering insights and observations on the game he helped shape.

Bobby Orr's flying goal in the 1970 Stanley Cup Finals remains one of the most iconic moments in sports history. It symbolizes the pinnacle of athletic achievement, a blend of skill, timing, and sheer willpower. But more than that, it encapsulates the spirit of Bobby Orr – a player who soared not just in that moment but throughout his entire career, elevating the game of hockey to new heights.

CHAPTER 5
The Magical Night of Darryl Sittler: Ten Points in One Game

Darryl Sittler is a name that will forever be etched in the history of hockey for achieving what seemed impossible. This is the story of the magical night when Darryl Sittler scored ten points in a single game, a feat that left fans and fellow players in awe.

Darryl Sittler, born on September 18, 1950, in Kitchener, Ontario, grew up with a burning passion for hockey. From the chilly mornings on frozen ponds to the competitive games in local leagues, Sittler's love for the sport was evident. He wasn't just playing; he was living and breathing hockey, dreaming of one day making his mark in the National Hockey League (NHL).

Sittler's journey to NHL stardom began when he was drafted by the Toronto Maple Leafs in 1970. He quickly became a key player for the team, known for his skillful play, leadership, and unrelenting dedication. Sittler was not just a player; he was a captain, a role model, and the heart of the Maple Leafs.

On the night of February 7, 1976, something remarkable unfolded at the Maple Leaf Gardens, the historic arena that was a temple for hockey fans. The Maple Leafs were set to face the Boston Bruins, a formidable opponent. Fans filled the stands, the air buzzing with anticipation, unaware that they were about to witness a monumental chapter in hockey history.

As the game began, Sittler was like any other player on the ice, focused and ready to give his best. But as the minutes ticked by, it became apparent that this was not going to be an ordinary game for Sittler. He was on fire, playing with an intensity and skill that seemed to elevate him above everyone else on the ice.

Sittler scored his first point with an assist, a glimpse of what was to come. The crowd cheered, but little did they know that this was just the beginning. As the game progressed, Sittler continued to dazzle, finding the back of the net and setting up his teammates for scores. Each goal, each assist, added to the growing excitement in the arena.

What was unfolding was extraordinary. Sittler was not just playing well; he was redefining what was possible in a single game. He moved with a sense of purpose, his every decision, every move leading to another point on the scoreboard. It was as if he had found a perfect harmony with the puck, with the game, with the moment.

By the end of the second period, Sittler had already accumulated an impressive number of points. The fans were electrified, talking and speculating about what they were witnessing. Could Sittler break the record for the most points in a game? The anticipation was palpable as the third period began.

As the final period of the game unfolded, Sittler continued his incredible performance. He was everywhere – scoring, assisting, driving the play forward. It wasn't just his skill that was on display; it was his passion, his determination, and his incredible hockey sense.

The atmosphere in the Maple Leaf Gardens was electric. Fans were on the edge of their seats, witnessing a performance that was nothing short of magical. Darryl Sittler, with each passing minute, was not just playing a great game; he was making history.

As the third period progressed, Sittler's energy and focus never wavered. He was in a zone, a state where every shot, every pass was precise and effective. The Boston Bruins, despite their strong defense and skilled goaltending, seemed unable to stop Sittler's onslaught.

With each goal and assist, the excitement in the arena grew. Fans cheered wildly, celebrating the incredible feat they were witnessing. Sittler's teammates, too, were in awe, playing their part in what was becoming a historic game. They fed him the puck, knowing that on this night, he had the Midas touch.

As Sittler scored point after point, he was rewriting the record books. The previous record for most points in a single NHL game was 8, a formidable achievement in its own right. But Sittler was on a path to surpass this, to set a new benchmark for individual excellence in hockey.

Every time Sittler touched the puck, there was a sense of anticipation, a feeling that something extraordinary was about to happen. His performance was a perfect blend of skill, timing, and sheer willpower. He moved with an effortless grace, yet each action was filled with purpose and intensity.

Finally, as the game neared its end, the unimaginable happened. Darryl Sittler scored his tenth point of the night, a feat that seemed almost surreal. The crowd erupted in a thunderous ovation, celebrating not just a great player, but a moment that would be remembered for generations.

Sittler's ten-point game set a record that still stands today. It was an achievement that went beyond the statistics or the thrill of victory. It was a display of what is possible when talent, hard work, and determination come together in perfect harmony.

This magical night was about more than just a hockey game; it was a celebration of the human spirit, of striving for excellence and achieving something extraordinary. Sittler's performance was an inspiration, a reminder that boundaries can be pushed and records can be broken.

As the game ended and the fans filed out of the arena, there was a sense of having witnessed something truly special. Sittler's achievement was not just a personal triumph; it was a gift to the world of hockey, a story that would be told and retold, inspiring young players and fans alike.

The legend of Darryl Sittler's ten-point game is a testament to the magic of sports. It shows us that on any given night, something miraculous can happen. It reminds us that sports are not just about competition; they are about moments of brilliance that can elevate us and show us the beauty of human potential.

As the echoes of the cheering crowd faded and the lights of Maple Leaf Gardens dimmed, the magnitude of Darryl Sittler's achievement began to sink in. Scoring ten points in a single NHL game was more than a remarkable feat; it was a milestone in the history of hockey, a demonstration of exceptional talent and perseverance.

In the aftermath of the game, Sittler became the talk of the hockey world. Newspapers and television shows highlighted his incredible performance, with fans and sports analysts marveling at the accomplishment. Sittler's name was not just in the record books; it was on the lips of everyone who loved the game.

For Sittler himself, the magical night was a culmination of years of hard work, dedication, and love for hockey. It was a testament to his skill, but also to his character. He remained humble, acknowledging the role of his teammates and the support of the fans in his historic achievement.

Sittler's ten-point game was not just a personal triumph; it was an inspiration to aspiring hockey players. It showed that with determination and passion, one could achieve greatness. Young players looked up to Sittler, seeing in him a model of excellence to aspire to.

The impact of that night extended beyond Sittler and the Maple Leafs. It captured the imagination of the sports world, showcasing the excitement and unpredictability of hockey. It was a reminder of why sports are so captivating: they offer moments of pure brilliance, where athletes transcend expectations and achieve the extraordinary.

Years later, Sittler's record still stands as a high watermark in the NHL, a goal that many have aspired to but none have reached. It remains a symbol of what is possible in the realm of sports, a benchmark of individual achievement.

As we reflect on the magical night of Darryl Sittler, we are reminded of the power of sports to inspire and amaze. Sittler's ten-point game is not just a statistic; it's a story of resilience, talent, and the relentless pursuit of greatness. It's a story that resonates with anyone who has ever dared to dream big and strive for the extraordinary.

Darryl Sittler's legacy in hockey is about more than just a record-setting game. It's about the impact he had on the sport, the way he inspired those who watched him play, and the mark he left on the hearts of hockey fans. His story is a testament to the enduring spirit of sportsmanship and the incredible feats that can be achieved when skill, dedication, and passion come together.

CHAPTER 6
Willie O'Ree: Breaking the Ice - Hockey's Color Barrier

There are some individuals whose impact goes beyond the hockey rink, transcending the sport and becoming symbols of change and progress. One such individual is Willie O'Ree, a trailblazing athlete who broke the color barrier in professional hockey, opening doors and inspiring generations.

Willie O'Ree was born on October 15, 1935, in Fredericton, New Brunswick, Canada. Growing up in a large family, O'Ree developed a love for hockey at a young age. He would spend countless hours on the local rinks and ponds, honing his skills and nurturing his passion for the game. In these early days, O'Ree's dream was like that of many young hockey enthusiasts: to play in the National Hockey League (NHL), the pinnacle of professional hockey.

However, O'Ree's journey toward his dream was fraught with challenges that went beyond the physical demands of the sport. As a Black player in a predominantly white sport, O'Ree faced barriers and prejudices that few others had to confront. But with determination and resilience, he persevered, driven by his love for hockey and his unyielding desire to succeed.

O'Ree's talent on the ice was undeniable. He was a skilled player, known for his speed, agility, and scoring ability. His skills eventually caught the attention of the NHL, and in 1958, O'Ree made history. He was called up to play for the Boston Bruins in a game against the Montreal Canadiens, becoming the first Black player to compete in the NHL.

This historic moment was not just a personal achievement for O'Ree; it was a landmark event in the sport of hockey. O'Ree had broken the color barrier, challenging the norms and opening the door for future players of diverse backgrounds. His debut was a step forward not only for hockey but for sports as a whole, signaling a move towards greater inclusivity and diversity.

O'Ree's entry into the NHL was met with mixed reactions. While many celebrated his achievement, he also faced hostility and racism, both on and off the ice. Despite these challenges, O'Ree remained focused on his game, displaying a level of courage and dignity that earned him respect and admiration.

Playing in the NHL, O'Ree faced obstacles that extended beyond the physical demands of the sport. He had to navigate a world that was often unwelcoming and harsh. But O'Ree's strength of character shone through. He handled the pressure with grace, using his platform to advocate for change and to inspire others.

O'Ree's time in the NHL, while groundbreaking, was just one part of his broader impact on hockey. He became a symbol of perseverance and a beacon of hope for many aspiring athletes who faced their own barriers. His story was a powerful reminder that talent and determination can overcome even the toughest obstacles.

Willie O'Ree's presence in the NHL was more than just a remarkable athletic achievement; it was a significant step in the ongoing struggle for racial equality in sports. His courage in the face of adversity and discrimination paved the way for future generations of hockey players from diverse backgrounds.

Despite the challenges, O'Ree's passion for hockey never waned. He continued to play the game he loved with enthusiasm and skill. His ability to maintain focus and perform at a high level, even under immense pressure, was a testament to his strength both as a player and as a person.

O'Ree's impact on the ice was significant, but it was his off-ice contributions that truly cemented his legacy. He became an ambassador for the sport, working tirelessly to promote hockey in communities that had traditionally been underrepresented in the game. O'Ree understood the power of hockey to bring people together, to teach valuable life lessons about teamwork, perseverance, and respect.

One of the most remarkable aspects of O'Ree's story is his commitment to youth and community. He dedicated much of his life to mentoring young players, encouraging them to pursue their dreams, regardless of the obstacles they might face. O'Ree's message was one of hope and inclusion, emphasizing that hockey should be a sport for everyone.

O'Ree's efforts to grow the game among diverse communities involved numerous initiatives, including hockey clinics, speaking engagements, and participation in various youth programs. His work aimed to make hockey more accessible and welcoming, breaking down barriers and fostering a love for the sport among children of all backgrounds.

The legacy of Willie O'Ree extends far beyond his statistical achievements in the NHL. He is remembered as a pioneer, a role model, and a change-maker. His journey broke the color barrier in hockey, challenging and changing the narrative around who could play and excel in the sport.

O'Ree's story is not just about overcoming racial barriers; it's about challenging and changing perceptions. He showed that the love for hockey transcends race and that talent and passion should be the only determining factors in the sport. His legacy is a powerful reminder of the importance of diversity and inclusion in sports and beyond.

As we reflect on the life and career of Willie O'Ree, we are reminded of the profound impact one individual can have. His story inspires us to pursue our passions, stand up against injustice, and work towards creating a more inclusive and equitable world.

Willie O'Ree's contributions to hockey and society have been recognized in various ways, including his induction into the Hockey Hall of Fame. This honor is a fitting tribute to a man who not only excelled in his sport but also used his platform to advocate for change and inspire future generations.

The journey of Willie O'Ree is a beacon of inspiration, not just within the world of hockey, but far beyond it. His perseverance in the face of adversity, his dedication to the game, and his commitment to breaking down barriers have left an indelible mark on the sport and its fans.

O'Ree's story is particularly impactful for young athletes who see in him a role model of resilience and courage. His experience shows that while the path to achieving one's dreams can be fraught with challenges, these obstacles can be overcome with determination and a steadfast belief in oneself.

Beyond his achievements on the ice, O'Ree's legacy is profoundly felt in the communities he touched. Through his outreach work, he has inspired countless young people to embrace the sport of hockey, fostering a more inclusive and diverse environment within the game. His efforts have helped to ensure that the joy and lessons of hockey are accessible to all, regardless of race or background.

The significance of Willie O'Ree breaking the color barrier in hockey cannot be overstated. It was a pivotal moment in the sport's history, symbolizing progress not only in hockey but in the broader struggle for racial equality. O'Ree's courage in the face of racism and discrimination paved the way for other players of color, creating a more diverse and inclusive sport.

O'Ree's impact on hockey is also a reminder of the power of sports to bring about social change. Athletes like O'Ree, who not only excel in their sport but also stand up for what is right, play a crucial role in shaping a more equitable and just society. They show that sports can be a platform for challenging injustices and promoting understanding and respect among people from different backgrounds.

CHAPTER 7
The Courage of Mario Lemieux: Triumph Over Adversity

In the galaxy of hockey stars, some shine with a light that is unmistakable. One such star is Mario Lemieux, a player whose journey through the sport is a testament to courage, resilience, and the indomitable human spirit. His story is not just about triumphs on the ice; it's about overcoming challenges that would have sidelined most others, making his achievements all the more remarkable.

Mario Lemieux, born on October 5, 1965, in Montreal, Quebec, was a hockey prodigy from a young age. His talent was apparent from the moment he first laced up his skates and hit the ice. He had an extraordinary ability to control the puck, a knack for scoring, and a level of grace that made even the most difficult plays seem effortless.

Lemieux's journey to hockey stardom began in earnest when he was drafted first overall by the Pittsburgh Penguins in the 1984 NHL Entry Draft. This was a pivotal moment for both Lemieux and the Penguins. The team was struggling, both on the ice and financially, and they were in desperate need of a savior. Lemieux was seen as that savior, a player who could turn the franchise around.

From his very first game in the NHL, Lemieux's impact was immediate and profound. He scored a goal on his first shift, setting the tone for what would be an extraordinary career. His combination of size, skill, and intelligence on the ice made him a formidable opponent. He could score goals with a deft touch, set up teammates with precise passes, and dominate games in a way few others could.

As Lemieux's career progressed, he brought the Penguins from the depths of the league standings to the pinnacle of the hockey world. He was not just a player; he was a leader, a captain who led by example and inspired his teammates to greater heights. Under his guidance, the Penguins became one of the most exciting and successful teams in the NHL.

However, Lemieux's journey was not without its challenges. In 1993, at the height of his career, Lemieux was diagnosed with Hodgkin's lymphoma, a form of cancer. This was a devastating blow, not just to Lemieux but to the entire hockey world. Here was one of the game's greatest players, in the prime of his career, facing a life-threatening illness.

Lemieux's response to this challenge was nothing short of inspirational. He approached his treatment with the same determination and focus that he brought to the ice. His courage in the face of such adversity was a beacon of hope and strength, not just for himself but for others facing similar battles.

Remarkably, Lemieux returned to the ice on the same day he received his last radiation treatment. This comeback was more than just a return to the sport he loved; it was a symbol of his unyielding spirit, a testament to his refusal to let adversity defeat him.

Mario Lemieux's return to the ice after battling cancer was a moment that transcended sports. It was a story of human resilience and courage, inspiring not just hockey fans, but people around the world. When Lemieux stepped back onto the rink, it was a victory not only against a formidable opponent in hockey but also against a personal challenge that tested his strength and resolve.

The day Lemieux returned, the arena was charged with emotion. Fans, teammates, and even opponents gave him a standing ovation, recognizing the immense journey he had undergone. It was a moment that highlighted the deep connection between athletes and their supporters, a shared understanding of the trials and triumphs that define the human experience.

As Lemieux resumed playing, it was clear that his battle with cancer had not diminished his love for the game or his exceptional skills on the ice. He played with a renewed vigor, a testament to his passion for hockey. His ability to overcome such a significant health challenge and return to play at the highest level was nothing short of remarkable.

Lemieux's comeback season was a display of excellence. He dominated games with his scoring and playmaking, reminding everyone of his extraordinary talent. What made this achievement even more impressive was the knowledge of what he had endured to get back to this point. Lemieux was not just a great hockey player; he was a symbol of perseverance and determination.

Beyond his achievements on the ice, Lemieux's journey had a profound impact on raising awareness about cancer. He became an advocate for cancer research and support, using his platform to help others. His experience brought attention to the importance of cancer treatment and research, inspiring many to contribute to the cause.

Lemieux's influence extended beyond his role as a player. In 1999, facing health issues and the physical toll of his career, Lemieux retired from playing. However, his love for hockey and the Pittsburgh Penguins remained strong. In a twist that few could have predicted, Lemieux became an owner of the Penguins, ensuring the survival of the team he had once led on the ice.

In his role as an owner, Lemieux continued to shape the future of the Penguins and the NHL. His unique perspective as a former player and a current owner brought a valuable viewpoint to the sport. Under his guidance, the Penguins remained a competitive and successful team, continuing the legacy that Lemieux had helped build.

Lemieux's story is a powerful reminder of the strength of the human spirit in the face of adversity. His journey through triumphs and challenges, both on and off the ice, is a testament to his character. He showed that with courage, dedication, and a positive mindset, obstacles can be overcome, and greatness can be achieved.

Mario Lemieux's story is not just about his achievements in hockey; it's about his journey through adversity and his remarkable ability to inspire others. His return to the ice after battling cancer and his continued success in the NHL served as a beacon of hope and strength to people facing their own challenges, both within and outside the world of sports.

Even after retiring as a player, Lemieux's legacy in the NHL continued to grow. His transition from a star player to a successful team owner was unprecedented and demonstrated his deep understanding of the game and his commitment to the sport he loved. His leadership off the ice ensured that the Pittsburgh Penguins remained a top-tier team, continuing the legacy he had helped build as a player.

Lemieux's courage in the face of health challenges also highlighted the importance of resilience, both physically and mentally. His ability to overcome significant obstacles and return to peak performance is a testament to his mental fortitude and determination. He became a role model not just for aspiring athletes, but for anyone facing difficulties, showing that with perseverance and a positive attitude, it is possible to overcome seemingly insurmountable odds.

Throughout his career, Lemieux's impact on hockey was immeasurable. He was not just a skilled player; he was an innovator on the ice, known for his creativity, vision, and scoring ability. His style of play influenced a generation of hockey players, and his legacy continues to inspire future stars of the sport.

Lemieux's story also underscores the importance of giving back and using one's platform for the greater good. His involvement in cancer research and his efforts to support those affected by the disease have made a significant impact. He used his experiences and his status as a public figure to raise awareness and funds for a cause close to his heart, showing that athletes can play a vital role in addressing important societal issues.

CHAPTER 8
Hayley Wickenheiser:
A Trailblazer on Ice

Born on August 12, 1978, in Shaunavon, Saskatchewan, Canada, Hayley Wickenheiser grew up with a deep passion for hockey. From a young age, it was clear that she had a natural affinity for the game. In the cold Canadian winters, Wickenheiser could be found on the frozen ponds and rinks, where she honed her skills, fueled by a love for the sport that knew no bounds.

Wickenheiser's journey in hockey began in a time when opportunities for girls in the sport were limited. Hockey, traditionally a male-dominated sport, was not always welcoming to female players. But Wickenheiser, undeterred by these challenges, was determined to play the game she loved at the highest level possible.

Her talent on the ice was undeniable. Wickenheiser possessed a remarkable combination of skill, speed, and hockey intelligence. She played the game with intensity and grace, demonstrating a level of prowess that made it clear she was destined for greatness.

Wickenheiser's breakthrough came when she became the first female hockey player to represent Canada in the International Ice Hockey Federation (IIHF) World Championship. This achievement was not just a personal milestone for Wickenheiser; it was a groundbreaking moment for women's hockey. She was paving the way for future generations of female players, showing that talent and dedication know no gender.

As Wickenheiser's career progressed, her list of achievements grew. She represented Canada in the Winter Olympics, where her performance was nothing short of spectacular. Wickenheiser wasn't just participating in these games; she was dominating them, leading her team to victory and earning accolades for her incredible play.

Her Olympic successes were a source of inspiration and pride for countless young girls who aspired to follow in her footsteps. Wickenheiser showed that with hard work and perseverance, girls could achieve their dreams in hockey, a sport they were once told was not for them.

Wickenheiser's impact on hockey extended beyond her performance on the ice. She became a vocal advocate for women's hockey, pushing for more opportunities, better funding, and greater recognition for female players. Her efforts were instrumental in the growth and development of the sport, helping to elevate women's hockey to new heights.

Hayley Wickenheiser's journey in the world of hockey is a story of breaking barriers and shattering stereotypes. Her presence in the sport challenged the traditional notions of who could play hockey and at what level. With every game, every goal, and every win, Wickenheiser was rewriting the narrative of women's participation in hockey, proving that the ice rink is a place for all who have the talent and the heart to play.

Wickenheiser's skill and determination on the ice earned her a reputation as one of the best hockey players in the world, regardless of gender. Her ability to read the game, combined with her exceptional athleticism, made her a formidable opponent. She played with a fierceness and passion that inspired her teammates and captivated fans.

But Wickenheiser's influence wasn't limited to her on-ice achievements. She became a role model and a source of inspiration for young athletes, especially girls, who dreamed of lacing up skates and grabbing a hockey stick. Wickenheiser showed them that their dreams were valid and attainable. She was a living proof that with dedication and hard work, barriers could be broken and new paths could be forged.

Beyond her athletic prowess, Wickenheiser was also known for her leadership qualities. She was a captain, a leader who led by example. Her presence on the team brought out the best in her teammates, elevating the entire team's performance. Wickenheiser's leadership extended beyond the rink as well; she was an advocate, a voice for change in the sport, pushing for equality and respect for women's hockey.

Wickenheiser's impact on hockey was recognized not just in Canada, but around the world. She became an ambassador for the sport, representing the values of hard work, fair play, and inclusivity. Her journey in hockey brought attention to the sport, helping to grow its popularity and accessibility for girls and women globally.

As her career progressed, Wickenheiser continued to break new ground. She participated in professional men's hockey leagues, once again challenging the norms and showcasing her extraordinary talent. This move was not just about personal achievement; it was about challenging the status quo and opening doors for other women in the sport.

Wickenheiser's legacy in hockey is one of transformation and progress. She played a pivotal role in elevating women's hockey, inspiring a new generation of players, and advocating for change. Her contributions to the sport have been recognized through numerous awards and honors, reflecting her exceptional impact on and off the ice.

The story of Hayley Wickenheiser is a celebration of the human spirit, a tale of overcoming obstacles, and a journey of making dreams a reality. Her name is synonymous with excellence in hockey, and her legacy continues to inspire those who believe in the power of sports to change lives and break down barriers.

Hayley Wickenheiser's legacy in hockey is not just measured by the goals she scored or the medals she won, but by the doors she opened for others. She transformed the landscape of women's hockey, proving that the sport is not defined by gender but by talent, passion, and hard work.

As Wickenheiser's illustrious career on the ice wound down, her influence in the sport did not diminish. She transitioned into roles that allowed her to continue advocating for hockey, particularly women's participation in the sport. Her voice became even more influential, resonating with those who make decisions about the sport at the highest levels.

Wickenheiser's journey is a powerful narrative that speaks to the resilience and strength of the human spirit. Her story teaches young readers about the importance of pursuing one's passions, regardless of the obstacles that may appear. She exemplifies the idea that with determination and belief in oneself, incredible feats are achievable.

One of the most inspiring aspects of Wickenheiser's story is her dedication to giving back to the community. She understood the importance of nurturing the next generation of hockey players and often engaged in initiatives to support young athletes. Her commitment to mentoring young players ensured that her legacy would continue to impact the world of hockey long after her retirement.

Wickenheiser's influence extends beyond her accomplishments as a player. She is a symbol of perseverance, a testament to what can be achieved when someone refuses to let societal barriers dictate their path. Her story is a source of inspiration not just for aspiring athletes, but for all young people facing challenges in pursuit of their dreams.

As we reflect on the trailblazing journey of Hayley Wickenheiser, we are reminded of the transformative power of sports. Her story is a vivid illustration of how sports can be a platform for change, breaking down barriers and fostering a more inclusive and equitable environment.

CHAPTER 9
The Unbreakable Bond:
Saku Koivu's Comeback

There are stories that capture the heart and spirit of perseverance, stories that remind us of the strength and resilience of the human spirit. One such story is that of Saku Koivu, a celebrated hockey player whose journey through adversity and his triumphant comeback is a tale of courage, hope, and an unbreakable bond with the sport he loved.

Saku Koivu, born on November 23, 1974, in Turku, Finland, was known in the hockey world for his skill, leadership, and unwavering dedication to the game. His journey to the National Hockey League (NHL) began across the Atlantic, in the Finnish hockey leagues, where he quickly made a name for himself as a talented center with a keen sense for the game.

Koivu's entry into the NHL was marked by his selection by the Montreal Canadiens, one of the most storied franchises in hockey. From the start of his career with the Canadiens, Koivu displayed a remarkable level of skill and determination. He quickly became a fan favorite and was known for his playmaking abilities, leadership qualities, and the passion he brought to every game.

However, in the prime of his career, Koivu faced a challenge that would test his strength and resolve in ways he had never imagined. In 2001, he was diagnosed with non-Hodgkin's lymphoma, a form of cancer. This news was not just a shock to Koivu but also to his team, his fans, and the hockey community at large.

The diagnosis of cancer is a daunting challenge for anyone, and for an athlete in the midst of their career, it was a harsh blow. But Koivu's response to this challenge was nothing short of inspirational. He approached his treatment with determination, a reflection of the fighting spirit he displayed on the ice. His battle with cancer was a fight not just for his career, but for his life.

During this difficult time, the support for Koivu was overwhelming. The hockey community, including players, staff, and fans, rallied around him, showing their support and love. This outpouring of support was a testament to the impact Koivu had on and off the ice. It also highlighted the unbreakable bond between a player and the hockey community.

Koivu's treatment was a journey of ups and downs, a period that tested his physical and emotional strength. Throughout his battle, Koivu remained positive, drawing strength from his family, his team, and hockey fans worldwide. His resilience in the face of adversity was a source of inspiration and strength for many.

The day Koivu returned to the ice after his battle with cancer was an emotional moment, not just for him but for everyone who had followed his journey. When he skated onto the ice, the arena erupted in cheers, a collective expression of admiration and relief. Koivu's comeback was more than just a return to the sport; it was a celebration of life and the triumph of the human spirit over adversity.

Saku Koivu's return to the ice was a powerful moment that transcended the sport of hockey. It was an embodiment of hope and resilience, a testament to his unyielding spirit and determination to overcome the toughest of challenges. The standing ovation he received was not just for his presence in the game but for his incredible journey back to the sport he loved.

Koivu's comeback game was filled with emotion. Each stride on the ice, each pass, and each shot carried a deeper meaning. It was a celebration of his perseverance, a symbol of his triumph over a life-threatening illness. The energy in the arena was palpable, with fans, teammates, and even opponents acknowledging Koivu's remarkable achievement.

The impact of Koivu's comeback extended far beyond the rink. His story inspired people around the world, from fellow athletes to individuals facing their own battles with illness. Koivu became a symbol of hope and a living example that with courage and determination, it is possible to overcome even the most daunting obstacles.

As Koivu resumed his career, he did so with a renewed sense of purpose and gratitude. He played each game with the same skill and passion he was known for, but with an added perspective that came from facing and overcoming a significant life challenge. His experience gave him a deeper appreciation for the game and his ability to play it at the highest level.

Koivu's leadership on the team also took on a new dimension after his comeback. He had always been a respected captain, but his battle with cancer and his return to the ice deepened the respect and admiration from his teammates and coaches. Koivu's presence in the locker room was a constant source of inspiration, a reminder of what can be achieved through resilience and a positive mindset.

Throughout the rest of his career, Koivu continued to play at an elite level, contributing significantly to his team's successes. His comeback added a new chapter to his legacy, one marked by courage, hope, and the unyielding spirit of a true warrior.

Koivu's journey is a powerful narrative about the strength of the human spirit. It teaches young readers about the importance of perseverance, the value of support from others, and the incredible power of hope. His story is a reminder that no challenge is too great when faced with determination and the support of a community.

As we reflect on the story of Saku Koivu, we are reminded of the unbreakable bond between athletes and their passion for sports. Koivu's story is not just about a successful comeback; it's about the journey of a person who faced adversity with grace and emerged stronger, both as a player and as a human being.

Saku Koivu's journey back to professional hockey, following his battle with cancer, is a story that resonates with themes of hope, resilience, and the unyielding power of the human spirit. His return to the ice was a victory not just for him, but for everyone who had stood by him through his difficult journey.

In the games that followed his return, Koivu played with a renewed vigor and passion. Each time he touched the puck, it was a reminder of what he had overcome and what can be achieved through strength and perseverance. His presence on the team was more than just a boost to their performance; it was an inspiration, a living example of courage and determination.

Koivu's impact on the sport went beyond his impressive statistics and accolades. He had become a symbol of hope and strength, not just for his team and fans but for people everywhere facing their own battles. His story was a powerful reminder that challenges, no matter how daunting, can be overcome with the support of a community and the strength of the human spirit.

The legacy of Saku Koivu in the world of hockey is multifaceted. He was an exceptional player, known for his skill, leadership, and sportsmanship. But perhaps more importantly, he was an inspiration, a person who showed the world the true meaning of resilience and the power of coming back stronger from adversity.

For young fans and aspiring athletes, Koivu's story is a testament to the importance of never giving up, regardless of the obstacles that may arise. It teaches valuable lessons about facing challenges head-on, drawing strength from within, and the importance of community support in overcoming life's hurdles.

Koivu's comeback and continued success in hockey serve as a beacon of hope and a source of inspiration for anyone facing difficult times. His journey emphasizes that with determination, a positive attitude, and the support of those around us, we can overcome challenges and continue to pursue our passions.

CHAPTER 10
Dominik Hasek:
The Dominator's Dominance

In the world of hockey, where goalies stand as the last line of defense, one name resonates with extraordinary prowess and uniqueness: Dominik Hasek, also known as "The Dominator." Hasek's journey in the NHL is a remarkable tale of skill, innovation, and a distinctive style that redefined goaltending.

Born on January 29, 1965, in Pardubice, Czechoslovakia, Dominik Hasek grew up in a nation passionate about hockey. From a young age, Hasek was drawn to the goalie position, a role that requires not just physical agility but also mental acuity. He honed his skills in his home country, developing a style that was both unconventional and effective, a style that would later make him a legend in the NHL.

Hasek's path to NHL stardom was not a traditional one. He began his professional career in his home country, playing in the Czechoslovak league. His talent was evident, but it was his unique approach to goaltending that set him apart. Hasek didn't just stop pucks; he did it in a way that was all his own, using every part of his body and often contorting himself into seemingly impossible positions to make saves.

The journey to the NHL began when Hasek was drafted by the Chicago Blackhawks. However, it was with the Buffalo Sabres that Hasek truly made his mark. In Buffalo, "The Dominator" emerged as one of the most formidable goalies in the league. His style was unorthodox, sometimes baffling, but incredibly effective. Hasek's reflexes, flexibility, and anticipation made him a nightmare for opposing shooters.

Hasek's dominance between the pipes was not just about his physical abilities; it was also about his mental game. He was known for his intense focus and ability to read the game, traits that are crucial for a successful goalie. Hasek could anticipate where a shot was going and react with lightning speed, often making saves that seemed impossible.

The Dominator's presence in goal was a game-changer for the Sabres. He elevated the team's performance, instilling confidence in his teammates and fear in his opponents. Under Hasek's guard, the net seemed smaller, the goal unreachable. He was not just a player; he was a force, an integral part of the Sabres' identity.

Hasek's skill and unique style earned him numerous accolades and awards, including multiple Vezina Trophies as the league's top goaltender and Hart Trophies as the league's most valuable player. These awards were a testament to his incredible impact on the game and his position.

But Hasek's influence extended beyond the accolades. He inspired a generation of goalies who looked up to him, admiring his skill and aspiring to emulate his success. Hasek showed that being different, having your own style, could not only be effective but could also lead to greatness.

Dominik Hasek's time with the Buffalo Sabres was marked by incredible performances that left fans and players alike in awe. His ability to make save after save, often in the most dramatic and unexpected ways, was a spectacle in itself. He was more than just a goalie; he was an entertainer, a master of his craft who brought excitement and a sense of wonder to the game.

In each match, Hasek faced a barrage of pucks from some of the best players in the world, yet he stood tall. His style, often described as 'floppy' or 'acrobatic', wasn't just for show – it was a carefully honed technique that made him one of the hardest goalies to score against. His unconventional methods, such as diving across the crease or flipping upside down, were driven by an extraordinary sense of the puck's trajectory and a fearless commitment to stopping it at all costs.

Hasek's influence on the game of hockey was profound. He challenged the conventional wisdom of how a goalie should play and proved that there is more than one path to success in the sport. Young goalies around the world watched him, learning that it's okay to be different, that embracing your unique style can lead to incredible results.

Off the ice, Hasek was known for his dedication and work ethic. He spent countless hours training, studying the game, and preparing for each matchup. This commitment to excellence was a key factor in his success and a trait that inspired his teammates and young players.

One of the most memorable moments in Hasek's career came during the international play, particularly in the Olympics. Representing the Czech Republic, Hasek's phenomenal goaltending was instrumental in leading his team to an unexpected gold medal in the 1998 Winter Olympics. This achievement was not just a victory for Hasek or his team; it was a victory for his home country, bringing pride and joy to fans back home.

As Hasek's career in the NHL continued, he further cemented his legacy as one of the greatest goalies of all time. His journey took him to several teams, including the Detroit Red Wings, where he continued to showcase his remarkable talent and contribute to his team's successes.

Throughout his career, Hasek faced challenges and high-pressure situations, but he approached them with a calmness and confidence that was reassuring to his team and intimidating to his opponents. He was a goalie who could be relied upon in the most crucial moments, a player who rose to the occasion when the stakes were highest.

Dominik Hasek's story is not just about the records he set or the games he won; it's about the impact he had on the sport of hockey. He expanded the horizons of what was possible for a goaltender, inspiring a generation to think outside the box and challenge the norms. Hasek's legacy in the NHL is a testament to the power of innovation, skill, and the courage to be different.

The legacy of Dominik Hasek, known fondly as "The Dominator," extends far beyond the many saves and victories he accumulated in his career. His impact on the game of hockey, particularly in the art of goaltending, resonates with a message of innovation, resilience, and the courage to embrace one's unique abilities.

As Hasek's career in the NHL drew to a close, his influence on the sport remained undiminished. He had set new standards for goaltending, challenging future generations of goalies to think creatively and push the boundaries of their position. His unconventional style, once seen as unorthodox, had become a source of study and admiration, a testament to the effectiveness of thinking outside the traditional norms.

Hasek's journey in hockey serves as an inspiring tale for young players. It's a story that highlights the importance of believing in oneself, even when your approach differs from the norm. Hasek embraced his unique style, worked tirelessly to perfect it, and ultimately changed the game because of it. His story teaches young athletes the value of individuality, hard work, and the pursuit of excellence.

Off the ice, Hasek was known for his quiet demeanor and humility, qualities that endeared him to fans and players alike. He approached the game with a professionalism and dedication that was evident in every game he played. Even in the face of immense pressure and high expectations, Hasek remained focused and composed, qualities that defined his career and contributed to his many successes.

For hockey fans and players, Hasek's career is remembered not just for the acrobatic saves or the numerous awards, but for the excitement and awe he brought to the game. Watching Hasek in goal was a thrilling experience, one that left an indelible mark on the memories of those who saw him play.

CHAPTER 11
Jarome Iginla: A Leader
On and Off the Ice

Jarome Iginla, born on July 1, 1977, in Edmonton, Alberta, Canada, embarked on a hockey journey that would see him become one of the most respected and admired players in the NHL. From his early days playing hockey, Iginla showed not just a natural talent for the sport but also a passion and dedication that would define his career.

Iginla's path to hockey stardom began when he was drafted by the Dallas Stars in the 1995 NHL Entry Draft. However, it was with the Calgary Flames that Iginla would make his mark and become a household name. From the moment he donned the Flames jersey, Iginla's impact was immediate and lasting. He played with a combination of skill, power, and grace that made him a formidable presence on the ice.

But Jarome Iginla's story is about more than his impressive stats and accolades. He was a leader in every sense of the word. As the captain of the Flames, Iginla led by example. He played with heart and determination, inspiring his teammates to rise to their best. His leadership style was one of encouragement, leading with a positive attitude, and a relentless work ethic.

Iginla's influence extended beyond his own team. He was admired and respected by players across the league for his sportsmanship, his fair play, and his commitment to the game. He played hockey with a level of integrity and respect that made him not just a great player, but a great ambassador for the sport.

Off the ice, Iginla's impact was equally significant. He was known for his community involvement and charitable work. Iginla understood the platform he had as a professional athlete and used it to make a positive difference in the lives of others. He was involved in numerous charitable initiatives, always eager to give back to the community and help those in need.

One of the most notable aspects of Iginla's career was his role in the 2004 Stanley Cup Finals. Under his captaincy, the Flames embarked on a remarkable playoff run, igniting a sense of excitement and pride in Calgary and beyond. Iginla's leadership was a driving force behind the team's success, his performance on the ice inspiring both his teammates and the fans.

Iginla's play during that playoff run was exemplary. He was a player who rose to the occasion, delivering some of his best performances when it mattered most. His ability to elevate his game in crucial moments was a testament to his character and skill as an athlete.

As the captain of the Calgary Flames, Jarome Iginla wasn't just a leader on the ice; he was a symbol of determination and resilience for the team. His leadership style was inclusive and motivational, fostering a strong sense of unity and team spirit. He had a unique ability to bring out the best in his teammates, pushing them to excel while maintaining a supportive and positive environment.

Iginla's contributions to the Flames and the NHL were not limited to scoring goals or making plays. He was an all-around player, known for his physical play, defensive abilities, and willingness to stand up for his teammates. He played with a sense of responsibility and pride that was infectious, inspiring those around him to strive for the same level of commitment and excellence.

Off the ice, Iginla's impact was just as profound. He was a role model, especially for young hockey fans. He conducted himself with humility and grace, showing that being a professional athlete is about more than just sporting prowess; it's about character, kindness, and giving back to the community.

Iginla's work in various charitable causes, particularly those focused on children and youth, demonstrated his understanding of the importance of giving back. He was involved in numerous initiatives, from supporting local charities to participating in programs that encouraged young people to engage in sports and stay active.

One of the standout qualities of Jarome Iginla was his ability to connect with people. He was approachable and genuine, qualities that endeared him to fans, teammates, and even opponents. His respect for the game, his teammates, and his competitors was evident in every interaction, earning him admiration and respect across the hockey world.

Iginla's career was also significant in terms of breaking barriers. As one of the few black players in the NHL, he was a trailblazer, opening doors and inspiring a more diverse generation of hockey players. His success and leadership in the NHL were a powerful statement against racism and a beacon of hope for inclusivity in sports.

As his career with the Flames progressed, Iginla continued to solidify his status as one of the premier players in the league. His consistent performance, year after year, was a testament to his skill, dedication, and love for the game. He was not just a player; he was an institution, a defining presence in the NHL.

Jarome Iginla's journey in hockey is a story of leadership, perseverance, and the impact one individual can have both on and off the ice. His legacy in the sport is marked by his achievements, his character, and his contributions to the community. He exemplifies what it means to be a leader, showing that true leadership extends beyond performance and into the realms of mentorship, community involvement, and setting an example for future generations.

Jarome Iginla's story in the NHL is not just a tale of athletic prowess; it is a narrative that intertwines excellence with integrity, showcasing the profound impact a dedicated athlete can have both within and beyond the realm of sports. His career is a vivid illustration of how a player's influence can extend far beyond scoring goals and winning games.

Throughout his time in the NHL, Iginla's presence was felt not just in the goals he scored or the games he won, but in the way he uplifted those around him. He was a mentor to younger players, sharing his experience and wisdom, and helping to nurture the next generation of talent. His approachability and genuine care for his teammates contributed significantly to the positive culture within the teams he played for.

Iginla's commitment to excellence was evident in every aspect of his game. He was a player who constantly strived to improve, to learn, and to adapt. This relentless pursuit of excellence, combined with his natural talent, made him one of the most formidable players in the league.

Off the ice, Iginla's contributions continued to resonate. His involvement in community initiatives and charitable organizations spoke volumes about his character. He understood the platform he had as a professional athlete and used it to make a positive impact, to inspire change, and to bring joy and support to those in need.

The legacy of Jarome Iginla is multifaceted. He will be remembered as a phenomenal hockey player, a fierce competitor, and a consistent scorer. But perhaps more importantly, he will be remembered as a leader, a role model, and a pillar of the community. His impact on the sport of hockey and on the lives of countless individuals is immeasurable.

CHAPTER 12
Terry Sawchuk: The Masked Marvel of the Net

In the history of hockey, there are legends whose stories transcend time, captivating the imaginations of fans for generations. One such legend is Terry Sawchuk, known as "The Masked Marvel," a goaltender whose skill, bravery, and innovation left an indelible mark on the sport.

Terry Sawchuk was born on December 28, 1929, in Winnipeg, Manitoba, Canada. From a young age, Sawchuk was drawn to the thrilling world of hockey, a sport that would become his life's passion and pursuit. His journey to becoming one of the greatest goaltenders in hockey history was filled with challenges, triumphs, and a pioneering spirit that changed the game forever.

Sawchuk's path to the NHL was a testament to his dedication and skill. He began his professional career in the minor leagues, where he quickly made a name for himself with his exceptional goaltending abilities. It wasn't long before he was noticed by the NHL, and he soon joined the ranks of the Detroit Red Wings.

In an era when goaltenders played without face masks, the position demanded not just skill but incredible bravery. Sawchuk was known for his fearlessness in the net, facing blistering shots with a calm and focused demeanor. His style of play was a blend of agility, quick reflexes, and an intuitive sense of the game, making him a formidable opponent for any shooter.

One of Sawchuk's most significant contributions to hockey was his role in popularizing the use of the goalie mask. After suffering a serious facial injury, Sawchuk began wearing a protective mask, a decision that would eventually lead to a transformation in goaltending. The mask not only protected him but also allowed him to play with a newfound confidence, setting a precedent that would become standard practice in the sport.

Sawchuk's presence in the net was commanding. He was known for his butterfly style of goaltending, a technique involving dropping to the knees and fanning out the pads, which was revolutionary at the time. This style allowed him to make seemingly impossible saves, earning him the nickname "The Masked Marvel" for his remarkable play and distinctive mask.

Throughout his career, Sawchuk faced intense physical and mental challenges. The life of a goaltender, especially in an era of minimal protective gear, was demanding and dangerous. Yet, Sawchuk faced these challenges head-on, displaying a resilience and toughness that was admired by fans and players alike.

Off the ice, Sawchuk was a quiet and reserved figure, but his dedication to the sport was unmistakable. He spent countless hours practicing and perfecting his craft, driven by a deep love for hockey and an unyielding desire to excel.

Terry Sawchuk's career in the NHL was marked by outstanding achievements and records, some of which stood for decades. His skill in the net led him to win numerous Vezina Trophies, awarded to the league's top goaltender. Sawchuk's excellence between the pipes was a key factor in the success of the teams he played for, including multiple Stanley Cup victories with the Detroit Red Wings.

Sawchuk's approach to goaltending was methodical and disciplined. He studied shooters' tendencies, understood their strategies, and used this knowledge to his advantage during games. His ability to anticipate where a shot would come from made him a master of his craft and a nightmare for opposing forwards.

Despite the physical toll of the position, Sawchuk played with a consistency and reliability that made him one of the most dependable goalies of his time. He was the last line of defense for his team, and he took this responsibility seriously, often playing through injuries to help his team secure a win.

Sawchuk's influence on the game of hockey extended beyond his impressive statistics and accolades. He was a pioneer, changing the way goaltenders played the game. His use of the butterfly style and the goalie mask inspired future generations of goaltenders, who looked up to Sawchuk as a role model and a trailblazer.

The impact of Terry Sawchuk's career is also seen in the way he changed perceptions about goaltending. He showed that the position required not only physical agility and reflexes but also mental toughness and strategic thinking. Sawchuk's legacy in hockey is that of a player who revolutionized his position, setting new standards for skill, innovation, and bravery.

Off the ice, Sawchuk was known for his dedication to his family and his community. Despite the demands of his professional career, he always found time to give back, understanding the importance of being a positive role model and an active member of his community.

As we reflect on the storied career of Terry Sawchuk, we are reminded of the enduring power of dedication, innovation, and resilience. His journey through the highs and lows of professional hockey is a testament to his character and his unwavering commitment to the sport he loved.

For young fans of hockey, Sawchuk's story is an inspiration. It teaches the value of hard work, the importance of adapting and innovating, and the courage it takes to face challenges head-on. Sawchuk's legacy in the sport serves as a powerful example of how passion, dedication, and the willingness to pioneer new paths can lead to greatness.

Terry Sawchuk's journey in the world of hockey, marked by extraordinary achievements and pioneering advancements, stands as a beacon of inspiration and resilience. His legacy in the sport is a testament to the power of dedication, skill, and the courage to innovate.

Sawchuk's career, spanning numerous seasons and teams, was not just about the games he played or the saves he made; it was about the enduring impact he had on the sport of hockey. His approach to goaltending, characterized by his unique style and his willingness to adopt new techniques like the goalie mask, revolutionized the position and influenced generations of goalies to come.

The challenges Sawchuk faced, including the physical demands of the position and the injuries he endured, underscore the toughness and perseverance required to excel at the highest level of the sport. His ability to perform consistently, even under immense pressure and pain, was a testament to his mental fortitude and dedication to his team.

Sawchuk's legacy is also marked by the personal sacrifices he made for the love of the game. His commitment to hockey was unwavering, and he played with a passion that was evident to all who watched him. He was not just a player; he was a student of the game, always seeking to improve and adapt.

For young hockey fans and aspiring goalies, Terry Sawchuk's story is one of motivation and encouragement. It shows that success in sports often requires more than natural talent; it demands hard work, a willingness to learn and adapt, and the courage to face and overcome obstacles.

CHAPTER 13
Sidney Crosby: The Golden Goal

Certain moments are etched in hockey history, capturing the hearts of fans and players alike. One such moment is Sidney Crosby's "Golden Goal," a shining example of skill, timing, and the magic of sports. Crosby, often referred to as "Sid the Kid," has a story that is not just about a single goal; it's about a journey of relentless pursuit of excellence and becoming a symbol of greatness in hockey.

Born on August 7, 1987, in Cole Harbour, Nova Scotia, Canada, Sidney Crosby was a prodigy in the world of hockey from a very young age. His talent was evident as he swiftly moved the puck and maneuvered on the ice, displaying skills that belied his years. Crosby's journey to hockey stardom was fueled by his passion for the game, his incredible work ethic, and a natural ability that made him stand out in every team he played for.

Crosby entered the NHL with high expectations, and he quickly proved that he was more than capable of meeting them. Drafted first overall by the Pittsburgh Penguins in 2005, Crosby's arrival marked a new era for the team. He brought a unique blend of skill, leadership, and a winning mentality that would soon transform the Penguins into a powerhouse in the league.

Crosby's impact on the ice was immediate and profound. He played with a level of finesse and intelligence that was rare for a player his age. His ability to read the game, combined with his exceptional puck handling and scoring ability, made him a formidable force in the NHL. He wasn't just playing the game; he was redefining how it could be played.

But Crosby's journey was not without challenges. He faced the pressures of being one of the most highly touted players in the league, expectations that would be daunting for any athlete. Yet, Crosby handled these challenges with maturity and grace, focusing on improving his game and helping his team succeed.

One of the most defining moments of Crosby's career came during the 2010 Winter Olympics, held in Vancouver, Canada. Crosby was part of the Canadian national team, a squad filled with some of the best hockey talent in the world. The expectations were high, but Crosby embraced the challenge, playing with the same passion and skill that he brought to every game.

The Olympic tournament was a showcase of hockey at its best, with teams from around the world competing for the highest honor in the sport. The Canadian team, with Crosby as one of its key players, advanced through the tournament, displaying a high level of skill and teamwork.

The climax of the tournament, and one of the most memorable moments in hockey history, came in the gold medal game between Canada and the United States. It was a fiercely contested match, with both teams showcasing their best talents. The game was tied, and as it went into overtime, the tension was palpable.

As the overtime period of the gold medal game commenced, the anticipation in the arena and among viewers worldwide was electric. Every pass, every shot carried the weight of a nation's hopes. It was in these high-pressure moments that Sidney Crosby's true mettle as a player shone brightest.

The game was intense, with both teams playing at their highest level, understanding that a single goal would seal their fate. The Canadian team, with Crosby as a pivotal figure, pressed forward, looking for an opportunity to clinch the victory.

Then, the moment that would etch Sidney Crosby's name into hockey lore arrived. A play developed quickly, the puck found its way to Crosby, and in a split second, he fired a shot. The puck, with precision and speed, found its way past the American goaltender and into the net. The "Golden Goal" had been scored, and Canada had won the Olympic gold medal.

The arena erupted into a frenzy of celebration, with the Canadian team and fans reveling in the joy of the victory. Crosby, at the center of it all, had delivered for his team and his country in one of the most pressure-filled moments imaginable. His goal was not just a display of his skill, but also of his ability to rise to the occasion when it mattered most.

This iconic goal cemented Crosby's status not just as a great player, but as a national hero. The "Golden Goal" was more than just a highlight of his career; it was a symbol of national pride, a moment that brought a country together in celebration.

Beyond his Olympic success, Crosby continued to excel in the NHL. He led the Pittsburgh Penguins to multiple Stanley Cup victories, establishing himself and his team as a dominant force in the league. His leadership on and off the ice was a key component of the team's success, demonstrating his ability to inspire and elevate those around him.

Crosby's journey in hockey has been marked by not only his achievements but also by his resilience. He faced significant injuries throughout his career, each time working diligently to return to the ice. His perseverance in the face of these challenges is a testament to his character and his passion for the game.

Off the ice, Sidney Crosby is known for his humility and his commitment to giving back to the community. He understands the impact he can have as a role model and takes this responsibility seriously. Crosby is involved in various charitable activities, focusing particularly on supporting youth and the sport of hockey at the grassroots level.

Sidney Crosby's influence in the world of hockey extends far beyond his impressive statistics and accolades. He is a figure who embodies the spirit of the sport: determination, teamwork, and the relentless pursuit of excellence. His journey is not just a story of individual success, but a narrative of inspiring those around him, both on and off the ice.

Crosby's commitment to his craft is evident in every game he plays. Known for his meticulous preparation and attention to detail, he continually strives to improve himself, always looking for ways to gain an edge over his opponents. This dedication has made him one of the most complete players in the game, admired for his skill, intelligence, and understanding of hockey.

Throughout his career, Crosby has faced intense scrutiny and high expectations, which he has met with grace and professionalism. His ability to handle pressure and maintain focus is a lesson in mental toughness and resilience, qualities that extend beyond the rink and into everyday life.

Crosby's role as a captain and leader of the Pittsburgh Penguins is a crucial aspect of his legacy. He leads by example, demonstrating what it means to be a team player. His leadership style is one of encouragement and support, fostering a positive and winning culture within the team. He understands that success in hockey is not just about individual talent, but about how well the team works together.

Off the ice, Crosby's impact is equally significant. He is a role model for young athletes, showing that success is achievable through hard work, dedication, and a positive attitude. His involvement in community initiatives and his commitment to growing the sport at the grassroots level demonstrate his understanding of the broader role he plays as a professional athlete.

The story of Sidney Crosby is a powerful reminder of the impact sports can have in shaping character and inspiring others. His journey is a testament to the idea that with talent, hard work, and the right mindset, one can achieve greatness and positively influence the world around them.

CHAPTER 14
P.K. Subban: Making a Difference
On and Off the Rink

In the world of hockey, certain players capture the imagination of fans not just for their skills on the ice but also for their charisma and contributions off it. P.K. Subban is one such player, renowned as much for his dynamic presence in the game as for his impactful work in the community.

P.K. (Pernell-Karl) Subban was born on May 13, 1989, in Toronto, Ontario, Canada, into a family where hockey was a cherished sport. From a young age, Subban showed not only a natural talent for the game but also an infectious enthusiasm and a vibrant personality that would become his trademarks.

Subban's journey to the NHL was marked by dedication, hard work, and an unyielding passion for hockey. Drafted by the Montreal Canadiens in 2007, he quickly became a fan favorite. His style of play was electrifying – a defenseman known for his speed, agility, and ability to make plays that changed the course of a game. Subban wasn't just a player;

he was a showman, bringing excitement and energy every time he stepped on the ice.

But P.K. Subban's impact extends far beyond his athletic prowess. He is known for his larger-than-life personality, his sense of style, and his genuine engagement with fans. Subban has a way of connecting with people, whether they are hockey enthusiasts or not, making him one of the most recognizable and approachable figures in the sport.

Off the ice, Subban has made a significant impact through his charitable work. He has been involved in numerous philanthropic efforts, particularly those aimed at helping children. One of his most notable contributions was his pledge to donate $10 million to the Montreal Children's Hospital, one of the largest commitments ever made by a professional athlete to a community organization.

This generous act exemplified Subban's commitment to making a difference in the lives of others. His donation has helped countless families and children, providing much-needed support and resources. Subban's involvement goes beyond financial contributions; he spends time with the children, bringing smiles and laughter, and offering encouragement and hope.

Subban's philanthropy and community involvement are driven by his belief in giving back and using his platform as a professional athlete to create positive change. He understands the impact he can have and takes this responsibility seriously, dedicating time and resources to causes he is passionate about.

On the ice, Subban continues to be a formidable presence. He plays with a blend of skill and intelligence, always looking to make the right play, to set up a teammate, or to score a crucial goal. His ability to read the game and his commitment to excellence have made him a valuable player on any team he's part of.

P.K. Subban's journey in the NHL is not just a story of individual achievement, but also one of breaking barriers and challenging stereotypes. As a black player in a predominantly white sport, Subban has navigated his career with grace and resilience, becoming a role model for young players who aspire to follow in his footsteps.

Subban's approach to the game of hockey is characterized by his unique blend of enthusiasm and skill. On the ice, he is known for his dynamic play – capable of making precise passes, powerful shots, and defending his team with determination. His energy is contagious, often igniting his team and captivating fans.

Off the ice, Subban's personality shines just as brightly. His sense of humor, approachable nature, and genuine interest in making a difference are qualities that endear him to fans and colleagues alike. He is not just a player; he is an ambassador for the sport, promoting hockey's values of teamwork, respect, and excellence.

In the realm of community service, Subban's efforts extend beyond his significant financial contributions. He actively engages in community programs, often visiting hospitals, schools, and participating in events that focus on youth development and empowerment. His ability to connect with people, especially children, is remarkable, showing a side of him that is compassionate and caring.

Subban's commitment to charity and community work is also a reflection of his upbringing and family values. He often speaks about the influence of his parents and siblings in shaping his character and his approach to life. For Subban, giving back is not just an obligation; it's a way of life, deeply ingrained in who he is as a person.

As a public figure, Subban has used his platform to address important issues, including diversity and inclusion in sports. He speaks openly about the challenges and opportunities in hockey, advocating for a more inclusive and welcoming environment for all players, regardless of their background.

Subban's impact on the world of hockey is multifaceted. He has changed the way people view the sport, bringing a fresh perspective and a new level of excitement. His style of play, combined with his off-ice initiatives, has made him a standout figure in the sport, admired and respected by fans, players, and coaches alike.

The story of P.K. Subban is inspiring for young readers, teaching them about the importance of hard work, perseverance, and the power of a positive attitude. It also highlights the significance of giving back to the community and using one's talents and platform to make a positive impact on the world.

P.K. Subban's story in the world of hockey is a powerful narrative that transcends the boundaries of the sport. His journey is not just about his accomplishments on the ice but also about his impact as a person, his leadership qualities, and his unwavering commitment to making a difference in the lives of others.

Subban's role in the NHL goes beyond being a top defenseman; he is a trailblazer, continuously showing that the game of hockey is for everyone. He stands as a beacon of diversity and inclusivity, inspiring a new generation of hockey players and fans from diverse backgrounds. His presence in the league is a testament to the evolving nature of hockey and its growing embrace of different cultures and perspectives.

Off the ice, Subban's philanthropic efforts continue to resonate deeply. His engagement with various charities and community initiatives reflects his understanding of the broader impact he can have. Subban doesn't just donate; he gets involved, he connects, and he inspires. His work, especially with children, is characterized by a genuine desire to bring about positive change, to uplift and empower.

Subban's energy and enthusiasm, coupled with his commitment to excellence and community, make him a unique and influential figure in the sport. He has become a role model for aspiring athletes, showing that success is achieved not only through talent and hard work but also through character, kindness, and a commitment to helping others.

As a player, Subban's legacy in hockey is marked by his dynamic style of play, his passion for the game, and his ability to perform at the highest level. His contributions to the teams he has played for are significant, showcasing his role as a key player in the league.

For young fans and players, Subban's journey in hockey teaches important lessons about resilience, embracing one's uniqueness, and the impact of positive leadership. It encourages them to pursue their dreams with determination, to be themselves, and to understand the importance of giving back to the community.

CHAPTER 15
Gordie Howe: Mr. Hockey's Timeless Impact

Born on March 31, 1928, in Floral, Saskatchewan, Canada, Gordie Howe discovered his passion for hockey at a young age. He grew up in a time when hockey was more than just a sport; it was a way of life, especially in the cold Canadian winters. Howe's journey to becoming one of hockey's greatest icons began on the frozen ponds and makeshift rinks where he honed his skills and fueled his dream of playing in the NHL.

Howe's entry into the NHL began with the Detroit Red Wings in 1946. From the outset, he made an impression not just with his physicality and skill but also with his humble demeanor and work ethic. Howe was a player who could do it all - score goals, set up plays, and defend his team. His style of play was robust and skillful, a combination that made him one of the most feared and respected players on the ice.

Gordie Howe's impact on the game was immediate and lasting. He was known for his incredible strength and durability, earning him the nickname "Mr. Elbows" for his tough play. But Howe was more than just a physical player; he was incredibly skilled with the puck and had a keen sense of the game. He could anticipate plays, outsmart opponents, and find ways to score from almost any situation.

One of the most remarkable aspects of Howe's career was his longevity. He played professional hockey across five decades, a feat that is almost unheard of in the sport. His ability to play at a high level for so long was a testament to his dedication to maintaining his physical and mental health, as well as his deep love for the game.

Howe's list of achievements is long and distinguished. He won the Stanley Cup multiple times with the Detroit Red Wings, was an All-Star numerous times, and held scoring records that stood for decades. However, Howe's legacy in hockey is not just about the records or the accolades; it's about the way he played the game and the impact he had on those around him.

Off the ice, Gordie Howe was known for his kindness and approachability. He was a role model to many, always willing to share his knowledge and experience with young players. Howe understood the influence he had as a professional athlete and took his role as a mentor and ambassador for the sport seriously.

Gordie Howe's influence in the world of hockey extended far beyond his physical presence on the ice. He was a symbol of perseverance and dedication, qualities that inspired countless players and fans. Howe's approach to the game, characterized by a blend of skill, sportsmanship, and an unwavering competitive spirit, set a standard for future generations of hockey players.

Howe's career was not without its challenges. He faced injuries and the physical toll that the sport of hockey inevitably brings. Yet, his resilience and determination to overcome these challenges were remarkable. Howe's ability to bounce back and maintain his high level of play was a testament to his strength, both physically and mentally.

One of the most admirable aspects of Howe's character was his humility. Despite being one of the greatest players in the history of the sport, he remained grounded and approachable. He was a true gentleman of the game, respected and admired by teammates, opponents, and fans alike for his conduct both on and off the ice.

Howe's legacy in hockey is also reflected in his contribution to the growth of the sport. He was a key figure in popularizing hockey in the United States, particularly during his time with the Houston Aeros and the New England Whalers in the World Hockey Association (WHA). His presence in these leagues helped to elevate the profile of hockey and inspired many young athletes to take up the sport.

The impact of Gordie Howe's career can also be seen in his family. His sons, Mark and Marty, followed in their father's footsteps, becoming professional hockey players themselves. The Howe family's involvement in hockey is a touching testament to Gordie's influence as a father and a player, showcasing the family's deep connection to the sport.

For young hockey fans and players, Gordie Howe's story is one of inspiration. It teaches the importance of dedication, hard work, and the love of the game. Howe's journey from the frozen ponds of Saskatchewan to becoming "Mr. Hockey" is a powerful example of how passion and commitment can lead to extraordinary achievements.

As we reflect on the incredible career of Gordie Howe, we are reminded of the enduring impact one individual can have in their chosen field. His story is not just one of personal success, but also of inspiring others, setting an example of excellence, and contributing to the growth and popularity of hockey.

Howe's legacy continues to live on, not just in the records he set or the trophies he won, but in the spirit of the game he embodied. His approach to hockey, marked by a combination of skill, grace, and toughness, remains an ideal to which players aspire. Gordie Howe's journey in hockey is a timeless tale of talent, perseverance, and the enduring love for the game.

Gordie Howe's story in the world of hockey is more than just a tale of personal success; it's a narrative that resonates with values that are fundamental to sports and life. Known as "Mr. Hockey," Howe's journey is a timeless reminder of the power of dedication, resilience, and the pursuit of excellence.

Throughout his career, Howe inspired fans and players with his remarkable skill and sportsmanship. He played the game with a level of respect and integrity that made him not only a great athlete but also a great human being. Howe's legacy is about the way he played the game, the way he conducted himself, and the way he treated others, both on and off the ice.

One of the most inspiring aspects of Howe's legacy is his commitment to the sport he loved. Even after retiring from professional play, Howe remained an active ambassador for hockey. He was involved in various events and activities, always willing to share his experience and wisdom with the next generation of players. His passion for hockey was evident in his continued involvement and his desire to give back to the sport that had given him so much.

Howe's influence on hockey can also be seen in the way he bridged generations. He connected the past, present, and future of the sport, becoming a symbol of its enduring appeal. Players, young and old, looked up to him, drawing inspiration from his achievements and his character.

For young fans and aspiring hockey players, Gordie Howe's story is a powerful example of what can be achieved with hard work, determination, and a love for the game. It teaches important lessons about overcoming obstacles, staying humble despite success, and the importance of sportsmanship.

Gordie Howe's story is a lasting legacy in the world of hockey and beyond. It's a story that continues to inspire, reminding us of the values that make sports such a powerful and unifying force. "Mr. Hockey" will always be remembered not just for what he did on the ice, but for the person he was – a true legend of the game.

Made in the USA
Middletown, DE
17 February 2024

49967356R00055